MW00354696

Beautifully Broken

Beautifully Broken

Shane Chase
Foreword by Daniel Aaron

Sunfyre Books, LLC

Copyright © 2015 by Shane Chase

All rights reserved. This book or any portion thereof may not be reproduced or used in any manner whatsoever without the express written permission of the publisher except for the use of brief quotations in a book review or scholarly journal.

First Printing: 2015

ISBN: 978-0-9903709-8-7 (paperback), 978-0-9903709-9-4 (eBook)

Sunfyre Books, LLC
PO Box 12024
Portland, OR 97212

Cover Art: courtesy of princessofpages.blogspot.com
Photography: courtesy of Leslie Todd.
Author Website: www.ShaneChaseWriter.com

This book is dedicated with love
To
Everett Slattery Jr. and Daniel Aaron, my soul brothers and the best friends
I could ask for,
To
Janiece Gilmouth, my guardian angel in the flesh
And to
My mother, Jeanne Goodin, who taught me the love of poetry and the power
of my dreams.

Acknowledgments

I would like to thank my publisher, Sunfyre Books, for taking a chance me, my editor, Matthew Warren, and the late CEO of Sunfyre Books, David Brew, for all their constant support during the publishing process. I want to thank Shannon Tower, my muse, Todd McDaniels, you inspire me every day, and Kyle Chase, I treasure what has become of our relationship. I want to acknowledge Ali O'Day, for a very special friendship and encouraging me to seek my dreams. I want to thank Leslie Todd, Teresa Anaya, Denise Hale, and Jeni Cleveland, the sisters I never had, and Laurie Mushet, you have walked me through many things and I am forever grateful. I want to acknowledge Karri Rees, for our special talks, Ray Henderson, Jeremy Gordon, Don Washburn, and Willie Nelson, for mentoring and guiding me on my journey. I want to thank A.J. Johnson and Dawn Darling, I will never forget the things you have done for me. I want to say thank you to Christina McCurty and Michael Hamilton, we are of the same tribe, Jason Minchey, my beloved friend, Yoli Legrave, for your support, and Karen Iliff for brightening my world. I want to acknowledge Katie Teasley for the inspiration for the title of this collection, and Samson, my constant companion. Finally, I want to acknowledge the owl and the wolf for providing me with wisdom, guidance, and spiritual strength throughout the course of this life.

River and Rain
Foreword by Daniel Aaron

Off he goes again,
The precious boy
With the tousled dark hair
And sparkling eyes that light every room,
Flecks of green, brown, and gray,
Off to his special place
Down the hill to the old oak tree,
A box of crayons in one hand,
Blank pages in the other,
To write, draw, create
A world of his own.

As happens in life
Leaves change colors,
Seasons change.

Off he goes again,
This precious boy,
His dark hair now styled
And eyes that sparkle from tears held back,
Flecks of green, brown, and gray,
Off to a different place
With concrete angels, epitaphs, and roses.
He traded blank pages and crayons
For a green spiral notebook and number two pencil.
To write, cry, and release
In a world of his own.

As happens in life
Leaves change colors,
Seasons change.

Off he goes again,
No longer a boy,
His dark hair tucked away under a navy blue bandana
And eyes that sparkle like never before,
Flecks of green, brown, and gray,

Off to a new place
With pastries, coffee, and windows.
He sits in the corner watching river and rain,
Using a moleskin and ballpoint
To write, dream, and share
A world of his own.

Preface
By, Shane Chase

I have been writing poetry for over twenty years and I honestly never thought these words would see the light of day. I must confess, there was a time when I didn't even want to publish my poetry.

The thoughts of a poet are deeply personal and, in my experience, achingly honest. We become naked and vulnerable in the telling of our truths. It can be frightening to be put on display in such a manner. That being said – when I was approached about doing this book, I was overcome and excited to share my art with the world. At my core I am a truth seeker, a romantic, a soul-searcher, and spiritually minded. I am a teacher, a student, a friend. My writing covers all of these subjects and more. In the following pages, you will find snapshots of my soul, pieces of my heart, and the thoughts of someone who has only ever wanted to love and be loved. I believe love is the essence of who we really are and what we are doing here on this earth in this lifetime.

In my life, I have had the wonderful opportunity to know some very special people. Many have inspired the emotions which, in turn, inspired my poetry. I share these words in hopes that you will take from it what you need and relate to it in your own way. Please let this become yours. It is no longer just mine. In this book you will find a journey. One of love and loss, spiritual bliss, self-reflection, and my questions of the world we live in. No matter how difficult things can be, I always do my best to find the magic in life. To be enchanted. I think this can be seen in my writing.

So, the invitation is this: to join me in celebrating what it means to be here, to be present and to experience all there is to offer in this place, at this moment. To embrace the idea that we are all beautifully broken in our own special way. Without further delay, I send this to you from my heart to yours, in the hopes that you will all embrace the idea that, in our own special ways, we are all beautifully broken...

Survivor

After the bitter chill of tragedy,
On the other side of despair.
One can only hope to make it,
But then life is just not fair.

A river of tears I've cried,
There are times when I want to hide.
Though I'm glad to be alive,
After all the times I wished I'd died.

It's all about survival –
That is the name of the game,
In time we all grow stronger –
Nothing stays the same.

I was so long buried by my sadness,
Hopeless was all I could feel.
Till I opened my eyes,
There is good in this world
And I know I have survived.

I am a survivor –
I've got to make it my own way.
I know I will,
I will find the sun one day.

Gypsy Woman's Dance

Tonight she debuts in all her magic
To tell us a story of her life so tragic.
Go ahead and take a chance
And watch the gypsy woman's dance.

Her crazy hair is a fantastic gold
And she is full of fire, so I've been told.
One may have to take a second glance
Or sadly miss the gypsy woman's dance.

It is said by some that she conjures the dark
And it's in this way that she leaves her mark.
You may see her coming from a distance,
Pay close attention to the gypsy woman's dance.

She is a lover and friend at alternate times,
You shall hear the bells in which she chimes.
Just be careful where you prance.
You may get in the way of the gypsy woman's dance.

She'll cast spells on you at midnight
And wind up laughing at you with delight.
You'll know she means business by her stance.
You would crave to see the gypsy woman's dance.

So come to the show and be sure to smile,
Don't forget to listen all the while.
You may feel you're in a trance
As you sit and watch the gypsy woman's dance.

Steel Tears

He stood at the foot of the stairs, broken hearted,
Feeling nostalgic for a love that could never be.
He couldn't even remember how it started,
Only that it ended in tragedy.

It seems the love I gave was never returned,
And you only watched me as I burned.
My love was buried in fields of ashes,
And my soul sacrificed.

Then, as always, I see you –
You look into my eyes and hold my hand.
To gently remind me of all I've been through,
And that I am strong enough to take a stand.

In the middle of my sorrow, you light the way,
Always there to light the way for me.
Guiding me passed the darkness,
And opening my eyes to clarity.

Though my sight is hindered by tears,
Brought on by the weight of these hurts and fears.
And all I put into those many years,
All I have left now are these steel tears.

A Space in Time

The sweetest eyes I've seen,
Caused my lips to quiver and my tongue to seize.
I fell hopeful, and youthful, and joyful –
Rejuvenated.

We speak and relate effortlessly,
I don't know what to do with that.
Except to react with a smile.

In only a moment's time, he opened my eyes,
Cleared the cobwebs that surrounded my mind.
Undaunted in the darkness and chill of the night.

He filled my senses, effervescent –
I clamor for his insight, and his touch.
Sweet emotion.

This sacred time – parallel universe,
He pulled me in like ocean waves, first soft yet intense.
The intensity of this moment, consumes me like burning embers.

He filled my space with such nerve-racking splendor,
And all he did was touch my hand.

No. My Soul...
He touched my soul tonight.

I Can't Believe

I can't believe the news you shared that night.
I can't believe you thought everything would be alright.
And what am I supposed to do with this information?
Your truth is a weapon and I've felt the blow deeply.

Am I supposed to just sit here?
And pretend nothing is wrong? Am I supposed to be forgiving?
The truth is, I forgive you on so many levels,
But I can never forgive the anguish you caused me.

I was supposed to be able to trust you.
Friends should never need to worry of such things.
I understand the free spirit you are, and the wings which help you fly,
Though I am untrusting of your reasons why.

Understand, I am a loyal friend,
And would never do such things to you, my dear.
Understand, I am evolved in mind, body, and spirit,
And will do what I need to free my mind.

It wasn't that I wanted to let you go,
I just can't believe, you thought I would stay.
Please be well in all that you do,
Spread your wings and fly away.

Ghost of You

Haunted by the ghost of you –
You were the only one who could really see.
And for all the trials and tribulations –
You inspired me and brought out the best in me.
Sometimes it strikes me that you are in the room.
Like a dagger in my spine –
Chilled by the light of the moon – as though a midnight tale,
But I know you are here and yes, I'll take your hand in mine.

Even as the cold winds blow,
I feel your breath in the candle's glow.
The ghost of you –
I feel you flow – right through me, you know.
If I close my eyes, I can still feel your embrace,
In the corners of my mind –
I can remember the tears, as they rained down your face,
And the candle burns,
And the candle burns.

Sebastian

I remember my first glance at you,
A face I somehow already knew.
A face so fair – I saw you standing there.
I listened to your story – you stood in all your glory,
Sebastian.

You walked with me down ancient streets,
Held me ever tight and promised not to leave.
And the first tears that I released,
You wiped them away with your sleeve.

The first time ever we touched,
Much to my surprise –
I stared hard,
Into Sebastian's eyes.

And the moment the crystal broke,
I knew the past had been left behind.
And only the path forward,
Was left for me to find.
Sebastian.

<u>Kings of Men</u>

You could be so much more for me.
I've known this from the very start.
And you could unlock the key to tranquility in my heart.
Where were you, when I was racing toward the sun?
Where were you, when I was restless and needed desperately to run?
Where were you then?

You were never there when I needed you.
I tried so hard to please.
I am often alone,
But your distance sets me oddly at ease.

Our spirits have wandered down wild streets,
Separated by our heart's desire.
Our ovations and our defeats,
I only wanted to be with you.
But even with you, I felt alone,
Now I find peace without you.

We must escape the pain,
If it's all we are able to do.
This dark and meaningless state we are in,
And remember the journey we've traveled through.
I know you know it's true.

We could have been kings of men,
But the dark clouds have come back again.
Like a haunted moment by a ghost passing through,
You know this is true.

Another day together, would mean more crying,
But we never said goodbye.
And this makes my heart feel heavy,
I would have made the sweetest love with you.
Now I send my love and say:
"Goodbye."

The Leaving

He turned and wiped a tear from his eyes.
He said "there is no more love for me."
Though he had known true love –
A love that even time could not trace,
And still he could not see.

There he stood, covered by the mist of the night,
With nothing left to say.
He knew there was no hope left in sight,
So, he bid his goodbye.

This was his dreamscape
His only escape –
Yet he only had the scars,
As proof of the love he'd once known.

Heartbroken.
Twisted and turning.
Soft spoken.

Always learning.
Broken.

He tried to smile as he walked away,
Knowing nothing could be the same.
Hoping there would come a day,
That they would once again ignite the flame,
Of an ancient love.

Tears were released.
Heart beats fast.
Soul bleeding for the feast
And no more love but in the past.

Grain of Sand

I think about you,
When the wind hits the trees.
When the ocean washes up on the shore,
When the night stalks me with a summer breeze.
Always leaving me wanting more.

When the sun rises over the land,
It's your smile in my mind that I adore.
And the soft touch of a grain of sand,
All of which leaves me wanting more.

I felt the deepest love and the greatest sorrow,
In the time we spent together.
I felt the safest in your arms that I have ever felt,
But with your love came stormy weather.
And there can be no more.

Please Sandman,
Take me with you, into your tiny dream place.
So there may be no fears that I must face,
Just you and I in our sacred space.

Yes, I can still be sometimes wild.
And to emptiness I am often prone.
But I remember clinging to my blanket as a child,
When I was so scared.
Feeling all alone.

Dare Me

So you think you can push me around,
You think I'll come running to the sound.
The beautiful sound of your laughter,
And forget all that followed after.

You think I'm sitting inside your hand,
You think I will fulfill your every demand.
You think you are my only dream,
You think I see you for what you seem.
But I know better than you –
The heartache you put me through.

Dare me to come back to you.
Dare me to run back and go on loving you.
Dare me to give you one more chance,
Dare me to give you just one more glance.
Dare me to share with you my innocent smile,
When I was only wasting it all the while.

You think I will bow down and beg for more.
You think I will come back through that door.
I know where you have been.
Dare me to admit you once loved me,
Or that I will ever see the way you see me.
Just dare me!

<u>Sparkle</u>

I know a boy who can sparkle,
He's got some magic in his eye.
See the dancing gypsy in the sky,
Hanging on cloudbursts in the air,
This boy is going to fly.

He's making gestures which are only known to me.
As he slowly drifts in and out of the night,
A haunting jester's tale but free.
And fast he disappears from sight,
To anyone but me.

But wherever he goes,
In the quiet he does cling.
There is a sparkle,
A tiny sparkle,
A tiny sparkle he does bring.

Some are never meant to stay.
Some just don't belong here anyway.
He needed fields to keep him free,
My best friend and soul brother
He will forever be.

And the last time that I held him
As he was lying on the evening snow
I just let him go.

With his sparkle.
With his sparkle.
I just let him go.

Cracked Open Inside

I am tongue tied and stuttered in awe of this love.
I missed you while we were dreaming –
How is it that we do what we do, the way we do?
You know, I already knew you the moment I found you.

You have me cracked open
Crashing lights against the great big sky –
As something happens to me deep down inside.
I need not even ask why –
A love neither one of us can deny.

You were all I ever wished for, this now seems so clear –
I've written about this and about you before.
And in your embrace, I feel no fear –
In the embrace of the dark prince that I adore.

In between our shared darkness and light –
We get someone and something to hold onto.
I will follow.

I've Grown Stronger

I built the bridges that they've torn down,
I climbed the walls but they've fallen down.
My crumbled streets they lay in ruin,
I need to get back on my own.

I fought so hard to make a start.
They made me think I was crazy in my head.
I thought I was long gone,
I fought my way back from the dead.

I've grown stronger –
And I feel guilty no longer.
To take a stand –
To take the truth and hold it in my hand.

I've been hurt and I've been burned,
But so many things I've since learned.
To turn around and hold my head up high,
Let out a deep and blissful sigh.

Never give up the fight.
I will win, I know it's right.
I am stronger than that,
Never give up the fight.

Obsidian

Every step I've taken along the way –
In quiet desperation,
Have brought me to this place.
I've persevered and stood strong,
You can see the melancholy in my face.
I must stay true to the things I want,
And what my aching heart may need.
Tell me why I'm forced to feel,
Tell me why I'm forced to bleed.
Confusing calculations,
And abhorring speculations are all that I see.
I see you and everything is right,
I see you and am reminded of the light surrounding me.
Still I can't make heads or tails of the world,
Turning around me.
I hold you tight and am grounded,
Every feeling is only a state of mind.
Still I am only hoping to find,
The strength my aching heart needs tonight.

Withdrawn

I am alone.
Solitary in my confinement.
Prison chains that are my own.
I am already gone –
I am withdrawn.

There is no safe place for me.
No oneness that I may draw upon.
There is no way to save face for me
When everything is completely wrong.
I am withdrawn.

I am in the clutches of the deepest despair.
I know not how to clear this stale air –
I am lost and scared, on this journey that is my own.
My fear paralyzes me before I've even begun.
I am withdrawn.

Even when the lights have changed –
And I am consumed by all of your lies.

And there are no silent cries –
I find I've been down this road before
And there is no rest in my heart's song.
I am here again –
Withdrawn.

Silence

Here I am sitting still.
These thoughts that will not stop.
In the quiet, silent moments –
Where all is still.

What I would give, to give everything to the world,
To the world which has given everything to me,
My health, my wealth, and my tools for survival.

I crave silence and yet do not attain it most of the time,
I crave love and see it everywhere,
I know I need silence for reflection,
I know I need love to survive.

At times I feel I have no voice,
And other times, I feel, I could have been the voice of a generation.
Does my generation hear me?

I am in need of expansion and realization of the power of my intention,
I am in need of a good adventure.

I crave to feel no guilt and hold no regrets,
And to let go of the past which haunts me,
Live in the moment.
I surrender to the ultimate spiritual kindred's of the world,
And I am much interested in the active involvement of my evolvement,
That everyone one day could speak these words.

These are my thoughts,
In these quiet moments,
Where all is silent and still.

Aidan

Inside the walls of your laughter,
I can hear the rhythm of your tears.
The untold stories of our past,
The reasons for our fears.
And the ways we couldn't make our love last.

Behind your smile – I see
The pains that you've confronted,
I can feel your pain –
A depth behind the surface, undaunted,
The water beyond the rain.

Life is an illusion –
Like a candle's flame.
I am searching the corners of my mind,
Only to find there was nobody to blame.
But it was love.

I reach out my arms to hold you,
And help you to question your pain.
To remember the beauty of all the rest,

To be wild but not to complain.
To become unhinged and each other to blame.
We will never be the same.

Remember the beauty of our love
Including the tragic parts –
Because there were magic moments.
Perhaps too many for our sensitive hearts.
But it was love.

Pleasure of the Pain

Caught up in the darkness of the night.
Wandering spirits in the middle of flight.
Washed within the waters of the rain,
Caught up in the pleasure of the pain.

A pain that strikes a blood red sky,
Pain that makes me wonder why.
Why the world turns its back on you,
While the pleasures we feel are too few.

A longing to make everything right,
Knowing we've hurt everyone in sight.
And yet there's an ecstasy about it,
And all the pieces seem to fit.

There's a pleasure about the pain,
A pleasure that could drive you insane.
And yet we feed off it all,
Which is why many of us fall.

Pleasure of the night.
Pleasure of standing in the rain.
Pleasure of the pain.

Alpine

On this misty morning,
I climbed the snow-capped mountain top.
I held out my hand,
To feel the falling of the dew.

Drenched in the naked snow,
The glitter covered snow.
Staring down into the dark crevasse.
In this place I feel free
And nature has a hold on me.
Something perfect in this world,
I feel safe.

The majesty of the silver landscape,
Offer a little blessing to me.
And the glacier – the spring,
Everything is beautiful to me.

Center of Silence

The path before me is clear –
I hold that there is truth in here
As I fight my way inside –
Where I have no place to hide.
From myself.

I came here to find
Soul connectedness –
A grounded, healing for my home.
To find this providence –
With solitude as my guide
I am not alone.

That I would find my center,
And the courage I constantly face,
I am craving silence again –
And consciousness.

I came here to find –
A workout for my mind,
For I seek traveling this way –
And new territories I may find,
Searching fearlessly –
Somewhere deep inside.

Beyond these walls,
And waterfalls –
I am craving awareness again,
This center of silence again –
And consciousness.

Quiet Inspiration

You are the gifted one beside me.
Releasing me from my fears –
The keeper of my dreams –
The shoulder for my tears –
You are always there for me, it seems.

In all my wild desperation –
You just stood there and held my hand –
With quiet inspiration –
Blessing me with your soul.

And you held me gently,
This beautiful soul –
Make me wise –
Make me whole –
I can breathe again.

The forces of the wind are with us now, love,
In the rain against the window –
In the thunder above –
He asks me to question my pain.
In hindsight, I've had so much more to gain.
There are no lies –
No heartache cries –
No true goodbyes –
Only the purest of intentions
In quiet inspiration.

Infusion

These are the moments I live for –
The freedom of my soul from despair, the liberty of my youth,
And triumph over the fundamental evils of the world.
To hold time in my hand, as though this were the last moment I lived.
Sanctuary in all sacred spaces, and all creatures of the world.
Breathe –
Water and air united within me.
This is the infusion of my soul.
Dance the dance and talk my talk, though not only words in form,
But rather the timeless echoes of my soul's vibrations.
Vision –
A vision of all humanity entwined as one, holding hands with eternity.
There is no danger to beware of, only life's passages to consider.
We could fly with the most beautiful wings and climb mountains of stone.
Meditate on you and the power of memory.
Never take a single moment for granted.
Stillness is the key and silence the key player.
Laugh –
You can change a person's day with one smile.
Learn to laugh at life and your heart will soften.
Nothing is unbearable and true friends will always be by your side.
Knowledge –
Life is a lesson, and the only thing which matters is
That you learned something from it.
Every step is sacred.
In the end – live in the moment, have no regrets and remember
Everything happens
For a reason.

Eye of the Storm

There have been storms all through my life.
I have felt the forces of the wind.
Never really knowing why –
Now I believe I understand.

No stranger to life's danger,
The chaos that surrounded me.
Hardly could I ever sleep,
At night I would gently weep.
I used to cry myself to sleep.

Life was confusion – as only a storm could cause.
Lost – caught up in the moment.
And it seemed as though others enjoyed it,
Perhaps that was only in my mind.

Now I know –
The eye of the storm is the calmest place.
I was the calm center amidst the struggle,
I made it through and found my place.

Was it ever really that bad?
I don't think so – I was only sad.
Though I am strong and I will go on,
If I've learned one thing, I know this much is true –
Every storm must come to an end.

Where Do We Go From Here?

Lost inside my prison walls,
A twisted labyrinth of my pain.
Driving myself to madness,
Going slowly insane.

I fear living.
I fear living in fear.
I fear the pain
Of living another year.

In all the ways we change,
It is so much harder to be sincere.
To what distance will we travel?
Where do we go from here?

I only wanted an answer,
I only wanted the truth.
Though the answer never shines through,
And we never really know the truth.

The answer lies only in the heart,
In the heart of someone who has been there.
And the only truth that is found,
We must go somewhere from here.

The Shadow

I am the spirit presence you feel,
When you think no one is around.

I am the creeping silence that fills the air,
When you think no one is near.

I am the ominous night sky that fuels your desire,
When you thought someone was there.

I am the golden dust left upon your shoes,
After a walk in the desert by yourself.

I am the voices behind your senses that you hear,
When you needed someone to talk to.

I am the true friend you wished you had for so long,
And never realized you actually had.

I am the man you saw when you looked up at the moon,
Because he was the only one to talk to.

I am the spirit that is always by your side,
I will always be one with you.

Brave Young Lad

He wanders the streets into the night,
Hoping some town will answer his plight.
A restless boy all on his own,
Into this world he was thrown.

Brave, some have said of him,
Though at times his future seemed grim.
And still he smiles and cheers
To forget the pain of all those early years.

An orphan in his youth,
People refused to tell him the truth.
The truth about his birth and his life,
A truth which can only cut like a knife.

He can only go forward from here,
He must not give in to his fear.
He will make his way one day,
And everyone that questioned him –
Will hear what he has to say.

Beneath the Surface

He turned to face himself again,
To search the deepest part of his soul.
What did he see?
What makes the boy a man?

Perhaps he desired a greater knowledge,
A lifetime's wisdom he'd long sought for,
And he wondered if he'd ever find it,
And then he thought – "maybe I already have."

He'd searched through diamond forests,
And laid down upon the softest sand,
And yet he desired more.

Faith is believing in something you've not yet seen,
And sometimes seeing is believing.
To what knowledge do we impart?
When we're not even sure where to start.

He knew he would survive it,
As all other obstacles before him.
He was stronger than anyone I knew,
And that was the only wisdom he needed.

Cigarette

We had many talks,
We intellectualized about life.
About things known and things unknown,
Of foreign cities and men we've known,
The cruelty of the world and kindness shown.
We discovered the truth of our friendship.
We talked over coffee and cigarettes,
Of the poisons we ingest,
And the knowledge that quitting would be best.
We agreed that we both have something to give,
I looked at him and said, "thank you, friend."
Shall we have another cigarette?

Comfort in Chaos

I have maintained this problem of self,
And a lack of inquiry into the essence.
Neglect of focus in itself –
Fueled by pain and intoxicating fear,
And I bear the scars of the consequence.

I found comfort in the chaos – all the time.
Alone, in my way – enormous mountains I would climb.
The barriers created – made of steel.
No stillness – that I might feel.

This has been my addiction –
Life centered in that of a storm.
This self-induced affliction –
And the many symptoms of this form.

Requiring myself to find another way –
I strive for tools and the ability to observe.
Knowing the price I'd pay –
And finding relief within this reprieve,
That chaos no longer serve.

Until You

In search of peace within,
And serenity of mind.
The oceans I have crossed,
And the mountains I have climbed.

There had been life without meaning,
Of little faith, unlike a rock,
With only sand to build.

It was then I asked direction,
I prayed a silent prayer.
I didn't ask for miracles,
Only a gift to share.

It was then the journey ended,
I knew the search was through.
Though the road was long and winding,
The path led straight to you.

Alone with Insanity

Walls caving in.
Motionless figures standing in doorways.
Groping for something other than silence,
Silence, oh sweet silence!
This silence holding me down,
These are the ties that bind me.
Can someone help me now?
I am the one in need of help.
Some call me crazy,
They may be correct.
The clock is ticking all the time...
Tick-tock-tick-tock.
Something has happened,
What are these tears?
I am scared,
Scared of what I do not know.
Of being alone, I suppose,
More alone than any can know.
The alone which causes death.
I only wanted someone to love me,
And I to love.
This should not be so difficult.
Where do I go?
I must go now,
Along on my journey afar,
To find myself.
Someone who loves me,
Craves me,
Feels me.
The one who knows and believes in me,
Faith.
Who honors my request
And wipes my tears when I cry.
I have always been on my journey,
Racing with the sun.
Yet I am still
Alone.

Faith Fail Me No More

I have lost myself yet again –
To the dwelling, the despair, the endless aching in my head.
Loss of prayers, smiles, and of love –
Just try to count the tears I've shed.
Everything is worth something, the price never too high.
That everything happens for a reason, and to everything a season –
If only a reason to try.

To see each magnificent sign of life –
A beacon of light upon the darkness.
So as to no longer feel the pain, and the aching within my heart –
To no longer be one with the darkness.

That I may transcend these moments –
It is a fact I have felt this way many times before.
That I may depart the ship of fools and learn the wisdom of the ages,
May it be that my faith shall fail me no more?

In Stillness

The chaos behind me –
Has left a void in my soul.
Though I have – willingness and I hold hope
That I would finally feel whole –
And I could finally cope.

That I would be able –
To be at one with me
And finally feel comfort,
In the stillness –
I pray – and so it be.

I'm stepping through –
In unknown places.
I'm not scared –
There are no traces –
Of fearfulness.

Here is my sanctuary –
And this is where my story begins.
I am not alone –
And there is much work to be done,
I am fearless.

I'm stepping through –
To the other side
Of what's inside –
The stillness.

Beautifully Broken

I remember the sun dancer –
Running fast against the wind.
We never even had a chance –
Under the weight of it, we were pinned.

Careless and reckless and out of control.
We thought we'd found beauty on the inside of truth.
But truth was too much for our sensitive souls –
We had tasted the bitter fruit.
And into the fire we fell.

We fell –
As if fine porcelain on a hardwood floor.
Crushed into a thousand pieces – were the pieces of my heart.
We were lost of what we were looking for.
And there was nowhere to go from here.

It was always you that I adored –
It was then that I came knocking at your door.
With many ways that I may implore,
Reminding you I'll be here forevermore.

You didn't believe me but then why should you?
After all, you've never believed in anything at all.
Your dreams had been crushed by the weight of the world we know.
Further down the spiral we fall.

I picked up the pieces of you and held them in my arms;
So beautifully broken, like the thousands of stars.
I cried to hold you for only a moment longer.
But longer is never enough.

Spirit Cry

The journey I am on has been arduous and long,
My feet are sore and my knees are weak.
I always thought I was unusually strong,
Now I wonder.

Have I not traveled to amazing places?
And seen the multitudes and faced their faces?
Have I not seen death in all its abnormal beauty?
I am stronger than they know.

I am a creature of wisdom and strength,
I crave the knowledge of the Gods.
Like the ocean that is never ending,
Still I wonder where we are heading.
Where do we go from here?

My spirit cries for universal truth,
My spirit cries to spit on lies.
My spirit cries to steal back my heart,
The heart that was stolen from me
So long ago.

Enrich me through the vortex of this life,
And I will carry the wisdom I attain, with me.
Hear my cry tonight,
Please hear the aching of my soul,
That none of us are truly alone.

For all these impossible things,
My spirit cries.

Fragile

I can see the heart that's breaking,
You're fragile as a porcelain doll.
Someone has torn your soul,
And the sadness which made you fall.

Tenderness in your heart at work –
The strength you possess,
Though hurt very badly,
The heavy weight of anger and distress.

Don't ever let anyone break your fragile being,
For you might break into tiny pieces.
Take the life blood from your veins,
And watch as your life ceases.

Fragile little girl –
You have worth to me,
Please feel sadness never.

To Have Someone

To have someone I can give my world to,
To have someone with which I can share my breath.
To have someone who I can live my life through,
To have someone I can hold until my sacred death.

There must be someone who shares my thoughts,
Someone who craves a part of my love.
One who can take what I have to give,
My feelings are scattered like the stars above.
To have someone with whom I may live.

I need someone I can trust,
I need someone whose soul I can share.
I need someone, whose love will never rust,
I need a smile that simply says: "I care."

To have someone who will whisper forever,
To have someone with an open heart.
To have someone who doesn't say never,
To have someone who need not depart.

The Ghost of Her

He remembered her tender kiss
And craved to hold her once again –
He cradled himself in sadness,
What has been done cannot be undone,
She brought him to madness –
She brought him to madness.

Years had brought them laughter,
Memories as vast as photo albums.
They used to count the stars –
Now he only counted scars,
For all the time that had gone by.

She left him during winter,
Eight years and ten months ago.
He is lost, he is lost, he is so very lost
Without her.

During hours of desperation,
He reaches for her.
To find the soul he is seeking,
Behind a wall,
Behind a door,
Maybe she was never there at all.

Until Now

I am numbing and averting – I am dying – I am done.
I am telling myself many lies –
The pain is venomous and consuming – sickness inducing –
Every time my faith dies.

Led by the force of chaos seduction –
Reduced by this self-inflicted will of destruction.
Not living my life for even a moment –
And lacking volumes of loved instruction.

Where do I go from here?
As I contain the shadow of my fear.

Until that day – as I stumbled upon this sacred place.
I can still hear you cheering me on now –
Wings of angels around my face –
Though the healing comes only quick as I allow.

To accept the love you've shared so free –
To finally be loved as much by me.

Today I am a part of the here and now –
I used to spend my time – being curious of how.
And I never knew the key to this –
Until now.

Anyone

I could be anyone.
Who would you like for me to be?
Who am I?
Not some stupid faggot like they all say to me.
I am a person.
Intelligent as well.
And I am a self-confident man,
At least that is the story I will tell.
I look in the mirror and see a face,
Handsome, young, and fair.
The only real problem,
My soul is in need of repair.
I have been hurt and abused,
I've been tried and I've been used.
I know that I can win this fight,
I always survive the darkness of the night.
I don't want to be anyone else,
I will work on myself until the work is done.
I will find and know me.
I am someone.
I am free.

I Love You

I love you.
Not only for what you are,
When I am with you.

I love you.
Not only for what you have made yourself,
But for what –
You are making of me.

I love you.
For the part of me which you bring out;
I love you for passing over all my foolish and weak traits,
That you can't help but see.

I love you.
For drawing out into the light – my beauty.
That no one else had looked,
Quite far enough to find.

Ethereal

Descending from a sky of clouds,
The magic woman suddenly appears,
An object of mystery for thousands of years.

An ancient queen she is called by some –
An old crone by others.
A healer and shaman in one,
She is called upon by her sisters.

Goddess, Queen, Witch –
Call her what you will.
A timeless beauty without a name,
Her magic amazes me, all the same.

Illumination

If only by the candle alone,
A burning flame and shadows upon the wall,
Dancing, dancing.
I can see the light.

With only this flame alone,
I am a seer of many visions,
Seeing, seeing.
That even broken hearts can mend,
Now I can make it through the night.

Dream Catcher

She is the one who sees me in my dreams –
In keeping with the stars at night,
She is eternal in her journey,
The keeper of my dreams.
Some called her a gypsy –
I call her the dream catcher,
Always watching,
Always waiting,
I flew through the stars with her,
We were magic in the night.
No one could touch us,
No one would stop us,
No one dared.
I stayed with her until the end,
As true friends do.
Sharing smiles,
I loved her,
The keeper of my dreams.

Vision Quest

Ready to take the dive and swim.
Spread my naked wings and fly.
Hope on the horizon and the sky is bleeding for me now,
Where will the wind take me? This is the question before me now.
Over ancient lands and vast seas,
Populating the sky with my tracks.
I am on the verge of something huge, and may not know what it is.
I only know, I want to go where nobody dares,
And learn the secrets of history.
Only then will my soul be free.

Trouble

Trouble,
Socked away behind my sad eyes.
A most difficult kind of feeling –
The madness and the stinging.
At first sight – betrayal,
Though for the sake of morality and truth.
I have shared things I have seen,
Now the time has arrived to come clean.
Down the long and twisted road of life,
Some people change.
The disillusionment is real,
And I am greatly effected tonight.
Standing here before the witness chair,
I nervously wait to tell the tale.
Palms sweating and fever burst,
Over lines I've not rehearsed.
Beady eyes gazing at me with subtle stares,
A cheap shot and a sudden glare.
I turn to you in frustration and say:
"I didn't sell you out my friend,
You did that for yourself in the end."

One Last Time (To Dance with You)

I called you today to spark a memory,
To make sure I could still feel you.
To remind you of the love I knew,
And remind you of the pain I went through.

I had not seen you for the longest time,
Yet you cross my mind all the time,
I needed to remind you that I am still here.

I've dreamed about you,
And had visions of you.
I've cried about you,
And all the ways you hurt me.

It all came back to me just now,
Like lightning from the sky.
To share untold secrets of the past,
Of you and of I.

You appeared before me,
Like the angel that you were.
Nothing had changed,
And yet everything.

One last time to dance with you,
To feel the warmth of your embrace.
You will remain forever in my mind,
An angel without a face.

If I Would Have Only Known

If I would have only known,
All the ways you ached inside.
I wonder if I could have saved you,
If I had only tried.

Did I never see you?
Or simply pass you by?
Perhaps I never noticed,
Did I ever listen to you cry?

Inside I always held you on a pedestal,
Though sometimes not out loud.
You'll never know how much I loved you,
And all the ways you made me proud.

You were my safety net,
A truest friend without fail.
I held the knowledge no matter what,
That our friendship would prevail.

There are so many things I want to tell you,
About how brightly you shown.
And I would have felt sorry for the way you ached
If I would have only known.

Midsummer Nights

The wind in my hair
Soft touch of sky
Summertime breezes
Pleases me.

Hand in the water
Feet in sand
Summertime feel
Heals me.

Rebirth at night
Bird takes flight
Summertime truth
Soothes me.

Light darkness
Cool-warm air
Summertime captures me
Suspends me.

Buddha Rising

Try to count the pieces of my fractured heart, they're beautiful, aren't they?

In their sick and twisted ways, lying naked on the ground before you.

Do you remember when you were thirsty? Barely thriving? I wonder if
You do.

I remember both thirst and hunger, something to sustain.

I remember crawling in seizure upon the floor – in slow motion, grieving
Living, do you remember this feeling too? I still think death is beautiful.

I remember, what it felt like to touch your soul, to lie naked with you in sweat
And to breathe in your fumes of lust and energy – life-force.

My dear friends, I remember too, the fumbling and the aching of our hearts
During these desperate times. These times of isolation and distress. The
Importance of it all.

Something happened on the way to Nirvana, something in the way we looked
At each other, no not an end to something but perhaps a new beginning for a
Buddha.

Enlightenment is a transcendent thing – come in out of the darkness.

We are all pieces of light in a world obsessed with darkness, but will all be
One soon.

This is the dawning of now, and the drawing down of the moon, seek safety in
Self and live again. I want to live again.

Let go of the past and make the present moments last, for we only get
One chance at this lifetime.

Angelina

O Angelina –
How your name describes you.
The face of an angel,
The voice of innocence –
You cast a heavy spell.
You move with tender grace,
When in the same room with you –
There is no time or space.
The bluest eyes I have ever seen,
The sweetest scent –
The most perfect lips I have ever seen.
There is a joy about you,
Somewhere deep inside you –
I see you working all the time,
Work a lot to earn a little –
Working for every last honest dime.
For so long now I've been observing you,
And I didn't even know you at all –
Though I know what I've said is genuine and true –
O Angelina, how your name describes you.

Prophets

Pour me a drink of your divinity,
Pearls of wisdom have filtered through to me in your absence.
I can only hold tight to possibilities now and am haunted by the struggle,
Yet sunlight continues to shine from your direction.
You speak in ancient tongues of things previously unknown to us,
I think you come from another place, a distant world.
Remember "The Days of Wine and Roses?" Drunken "feasts of friends?"
We were such prophets then and still we didn't know what we wanted.
What do you dream when you dream? Did the tarot talk to you again?
Mine did, but I drew the cards for you.
"I spoke with James Dean and he said to say hi. You know I commune with
The dead. Speaking of which, have you talked to my mother lately?"
How I desire to walk through the trees with you again, to talk of important
Things. And sing and dance and share, anything really if we care.
We can go anywhere. I always feel safe in your presence.
We need a magic moment and a good conversation.
Don't forget me ever, my love.

Conjure the Wind

He held his friend,
As if this were his eternity.
As if every tear meant one more year of his life,
What a long life we live.

They have traveled through portals of time,
Held each other's life forces in a vein,
Stumbling blindly as poets sometimes do,
There was magic in the night.

He said, "Do you know I can conjure the wind?"
"I feel it in the air..."
The rustling of trees.
The wind comes roaring up,
Like tiny tortured screams.
Sometimes feels like crashing ocean waves.
And only these two felt the power that moment brought,
Sweet salvation saves.

Hanging in graveyards,
Drinking coffee until dawn.
Living as Golden Gods,
Creating Art they've not yet drawn.
And words not yet spoken.

"Did you know I can conjure the wind?"
Feel it in the rustling of the trees.
The wind comes roaring up,
Like tiny tortured screams.
We held each other then.

December Five

I've walked with you down avenues of hope,
Through pastures of peace.
I've walked with you down diamond streets,
And watched dark moments turn into gold.

See the boy with stars in his eyes,
Gathering smiles as he walks right by.
Even in moments of desperation,
I never have seen him cry.

The truth is your identity,
I think this is important to see.
The truth that resides deep inside of us all,
For the truth shall set us free.

I love you for your courage,
For your strength in destructive forces.
This fire that lies in the center of your soul,
In a place you never even knew existed before.

We are constantly growing,
And when in your presence I feel no fear.
This beautiful soul that came to be
On December Five of that year.

Little Star

Little star,
Where have you gone now?
Please don't fade away.
You are so far away from me,
And I can't touch you anymore,
Little star.

Your flame burns bright,
And it burns fast.
And the mystery of you,
Consumes every thought of me
As you are taken within the sky.

You are elusive and fleeting and flying,
Freedom seeps from your sides.
I can see both sides of you now,
Like dual personalities,
And I trust you anyway.

Little star,
Where have you gone now?
I can't see you anymore.
Please don't fade away from me,
Little star.

Palisades

I've heard the mountains calling my name.
I've seen this river of truth in these quiet moments.
I've felt spirit in the distance flowing.
I've sought spirit in the present moment of all-knowing.

I can feel the synergy,
I am in this spirit energy.
Six hundred feet above ground –
This-energy.

I bow to this precious time,
Between darkness and soul bliss.
Between the past and a delicious sun kiss.

I can feel the synergy in the air.
I am in the agape flow and I am aware.
I am unabashedly alive,
In this-energy.

I am –
Thrill seeker,
Adventurer,
Student,
Teacher.
I am whole.

Sanctuary

I remember the chill of alone,
Standing in the cold, dark waters.
I remember the loss of spirit...
The black cloud of mystery...
That was a long time ago.

The cell that surrounded me,
I built that cell for myself,
And the pain we caused ourselves,
Though that was a long time ago.

I see my reflection,
Staring back at me.
I see how sad and desperate I appear,
Times will come and they will go,
None of these are easy.
We need to reach somewhere deep within,
And set out upon our journey...
Set out on the journey of this life.

I want to stand at the foot of the great mountain,
Embrace the wisdom of my guides,
And to hold my own hand,
No fear of being alone.

I see my reflection,
Staring back at me.
I understand now how I appear,
And the reasons I am here.

I still remember the chill of alone,
But I am not afraid of dark waters.
I remember regaining my freedom,
And the freedom of letting go.

The Tracks of My Tears

I thought I was in love with you.
Mistaken love it seems –
Though the light around you just beams,
Your brilliant mind captivates simplicity.

Never have I seen you cry,
Now I have to question why –
In the many ways I never saw you try,
It was a waste of a long goodbye.

Remember those long talks of heartache,
And that of our frozen fears –
Now I wonder if you still see my face,
I wonder if you can trace the tracks of my tears.

That you would be somewhere thinking of me,
That within your soul, you would be free –
The love we find must come from deep within,
And I know this is where my life will begin.

We have to be the change we want to see,
And I know because of you –
I've become something better for me.

We can hold these beautiful days,
These sacred moments,
Take the ugly things –
And wish them away.

Unbreakable Heart

You think you can call me when you want to dance.
You think I'll offer you a second chance.
You assume I'll just let you in,
But you can't tell me where you have been.

What is it you want from me?
Don't you know I wish to be free?
Free from empty promises and life's pain,
Free from your kingdom and your reign.

Share with me your deepest love,
And I'll offer you a love that is not fake.
But hurt me again and I'll show you
A heart that does not break.

Life is fragile and love is hard,
I cannot allow myself to give up my guard.
It only takes twice to learn the third time,
Drifting through the sands of time.

I want to love you and I do,
I guess I'm one of the lucky few.
To stand up and shout beyond the shadow of doubt,
That I know what life and love are about.

Share with me your passions and dreams,
And I will offer you a fresh start
And you'll find my unbreakable heart.

Beautiful Memory

I stared into his beautiful eyes and
He stared back into mine,
He always had amazing eyes.
The connection still visible,
As truth stands solid,
And yet I don't know what to do.
How he still affects me,
With every fiber of my soul.
The way the wind changes,
And the light reflects,
I am consumed with desire for him.
I don't want to need to want him,
And still I crave to love him.
I am feverish for his touch.
We can never be again,
Though in my heart he will always remain
A beautiful memory.

Shaman Woman Blues

She touches the body and it heals,
It comes from somewhere unknown to us.
Powers of magic and of mysticism,
She brings it all to the surface.

The woman closes her eyes,
She feels the current of the body's soul.
She feels and feels and heals,
To release the toxins of the soul.

Woman of mystery.
Her weapons are secret; her soul bleeds for another,
She bleeds openly.

One will never know the power,
The power she possesses.
She sings the shaman woman blues –
To us every day.

The Last Word

I heard myself speak,
As the words fell like liquid from my tongue.
Incoherent.
Unaware of my actions, thoughts, or words.
The many fears that bind me,
Cause my tongue to seize in my throat.
My eyes filled with tears,
As he spoke down to me.
What did I do to deserve this?
The mistreatment and the shame.
Perhaps after all, I was the one to blame.

Chasing Aladdin's Dreams

Amidst the sun swept sky –
And chasing my dreams through midnight fair.
A dream of hope drifting passed my mind,
And thought of another life out there.

Beyond anything imagined,
Anything these eyes have seen –
There is a kind of magic beyond the clouds,
Somewhere behind the scene.

Is there destiny out there?
A magic lamp that I may hold?
A glittering promise of wishes and dreams
Like every fairy tale that has been told.

May we climb aboard a shooting star?
Build our pyramid of dreams?
For our dreams may pass quite quickly,
When you feel your dreams are fading,
And everything has turned to black –
Remember the hope that filled you once
And you will find your way back.

Back to the beginning of the road,
You know it is never too late.
To find the beauty that surrounds you –
And fill your proverbial plate.

Heart on My Sleeve

I wonder if you ever heard the whispers of my heart,
And the pulsating thunder of my heartbeat
During the beautiful and silent moments we shared.
You came to me as a beacon of light,
The flame of a long burning candle.
And in the dark moments, stood before me in beauty.
Your absence has consumed me.
To devour your love completely,
And as we wept, I offered you my love sweetly.
There is a special place for you,
Within this heart upon my sleeve.
That you can see me for all I am,
And appreciate the love in which I strongly believe.

Still Waters

Tears wept from my heart,
As I sat and contemplated your majestic beauty –
But your tongue – bitter like wine,
Has caused me to seize.

This has felt like a dream,
Where nothing is as it seems.
Where there is no logic and time has no end
But endings can be beautiful.

You are well versed in the art of catch and release.
Pull me in and push me away,
Could you finally let me go please?

This is the reclaiming of the self –
Against the self-righteous,
And I am the messenger of my soul,
Relaying the message to the one who will not give it back.

Caught in holding patterns,
Against the darkened sky.
I don't know if you are aware
Where your happy moments lie.

You say you want love,
Well here it stands before you
In the form of my flesh.
And all the rest.

There are many tunnels I must travel through,
Just to reach you.
The arsenal you've thrown in my direction
Has left me bleeding within. For you.

You've taken me back in time with you;
You knew what you were doing all along.
I can't stand by to smell your flowers as they wither.
At last, I am through.

I was told not to worry though.
As this is only another lesson,
"At least you can still feel."
"At least you know your love is real.
I would have been your sole companion.

And I would have,
You thief of hearts!
I didn't think we'd end up like this,
I only wanted to break bread with you.

Faith in Nothing

She cried reckless tears,
For the parade of men who had been reckless with her.
She amazed me in her unabashed way,
In the desperation of the moment,
And the cool of her disposition,
I held her.
To hold a single tear in your hand,
And feel what others have felt before,
Even if different than anything others had felt,
I held her.
I told her sweet things,
I wanted her to know that she was beautiful,
I wanted her to know her life was worth living,
And she was capable of bliss.
Even after all the tears she cried,
I begged her to know life's beauty had not died,
And still
She cried reckless tears.

Reclaiming

Wandering – lost in the wilderness of my ancient ways,
Forever praying to be found –
From a template of love's inner empire,
I inquired with only a whispered sound.

There were no bolts of lightning –
Or loud bursts of thunder –
No crashing waves with promise of taking me under
Only a simplistic revelation –
The key to my self-salvation.

All I need resides within my being.
If I find it, then I will be free –
Catching dreams may be the key to seeing –
All that I need ever be.

My soul lies naked in the light –
The reclaiming of hidden beauty and of lost youth.
The promise of courage and conquering the fight.

Yes, it could be heaven –
And sometimes it was a nightmare –
I turned to see the face in the mirror,
I had to face my own fear –

This is the reclaiming of my sacred soul,
The truth lies naked in the light –
The reclaiming of my heart and of becoming whole.
The promise of eternal peace and insight –
Oh Great Spirit, please hear my plight.

Waves of My Soul

To understand my soul is to listen to my journey.
Of the oceans and mountains, down to the stream.

There has been much magic in my life;
And I have been touched by gold.
I will share with you...
But the secrets inside shall stay untold.

To record my autobiography would be epic,
For I am like the ocean – vast, deep, magnetic.
Both nourishing and nurturing –
And sometimes, in the evening, tormented.

Listen to my heart – the spirit that cries out
For nurturing, for love, for everything the heart desires.
My spirit cries for the things money can't buy,
For the victims, for the peace, for the spiritual.
And for the children.

The road we follow is so very long,
And I have been patient.
The longing, the yearning, the tears in the night.
We are all masters of something in this life.

About the poet...

Shane Chase writes poetry, short stories, and articles. He is currently writing his debut novel. Originally from Hood River, Oregon, Shane has been writing for over twenty years and has previously been featured in literary articles and publications. With a natural talent for the written word, he has the ability to connect with others on a deeper level. Shane resides in Portland, Oregon, with his cat, Samson.

CPSIA information can be obtained at www.ICGtesting.com
Printed in the USA
BVOW08s2011160716

455821BV00001B/70/P